Old Skene and Echt

by
W. Stewart Wilson

The Central Public School at Skene was built in 1864 and until the middle of the 19th century was a Junior Secondary School. The original parish school is said to have stood in what is locally called (from its shape) the *Fiddle Woodie*, near the line of the Old Skene Road and almost half a mile from the Kirkton. In the 1820s a Dames' school was established in the Kirkton, and another probably at Westhill. The Free Church had one school at the Lyne of Skene and another at the Mason Lodge. At Garlogie Wool Mills the company provided a school for the children of the workers. By 1955 there were four schools in the parish, at Skene, Garlogie, Lyne of Skene and Westhill. The number of pupils enrolled at that date at Skene (which at the time was still a Junior Secondary School) was 154, at Garlogie there were 38 pupils and at Lyne of Skene 34, and at Westhill there were 43. Today the three primary schools have been closed and been replaced by the new schools of Elrick, Crombie and Westhill, all in the Westhill area. Skene alone remains but is now only a primary school and Westhill Academy caters for all the pupils of secondary school age.

Text © W. Stewart Wilson, 2009.
First published in the United Kingdom, 2009,
by Stenlake Publishing Ltd.
Telephone: 01290 551122
www.stenlake.co.uk

ISBN 9781840334548

The publishers regret that they cannot supply
copies of any pictures featured in this book.

Acknowledgements

I would like to thank all those who have given of their local knowledge including Ian Douglas, David Jamieson, Eric and Jean Robertson, Ronald Smith OBE, Sandy Weir.

Further Reading

The books listed below were used by the author during his research. None of them are available from Stenlake Publishing. Those interested in finding out more are advised to contact their local bookshop or reference library.

The various *Statistical Accounts* of the parishes of Skene and Echt
The Deeside Field Club magazines
The Leopard magazine
The Old Deeside Road by G M Fraser published in 1921
The Coming of Turnpikes to Aberdeenshire by John Patrick
Grampian Battlefields by Peter Marren published in1990
Aberdeenshire, Donside and Strathbogie an illustrated architectural guide by Ian Shepherd published in 1994
Haunted Valley by Norman Adams published in1994
A History of the Parish of Skene published in 2001
The Road to Maggieknockater by Robert Smith published in 2004
Hangman's Brae by Norman Adams published in 2005

Introduction

The parish of Skene lies immediately to the west of the City of Aberdeen and until the creation of Westhill had as its centres of population, Kirkton of Skene, Elrick, Lyne of Skene and Garlogie. The adjoining Parish of Echt to the west is divided into three distinct communities grouped around the villages of Echt in the middle with Dunecht to the north and Cullerlie on the south. In 1925 an eminent local historian, W Douglas Simpson in referring to the parishes of Skene and Echt wrote *that despite their remoteness from the mainspring of action their story does not lack interest and value*. Their rural nature continued until the 1960s and a comparison of the population of the two parishes between 1901 and 1951 is confirmation of this. In 1901 the population of the parish of Skene was 1,546 and by 1951 had contracted slightly to 1,436. In 1901 657 lived in the parish of Echt and by 1951 this had risen to 1,028. The rise in the population of the parish of Echt over these fifty years can be accounted for by the increased importance of the estate of Dunecht. The parish of Skene on the other hand saw little change over the same period. Since the 1960s though there has been a dramatic increase in population with the creation of Westhill, on the eastern edge of the city of Aberdeen and a rapid expansion of housing and business development westwards through Elrick to Skene. The population of Westhill alone, as recorded in the 2001 census, was 9,498.

As in most of Aberdeenshire the earliest signs of civilisation date from around 4000 BC. Implements of flint and polished stone have been unearthed around Dunecht. Just outside the parish of Skene at what is now West Hatton Farm a long cairn was discovered which dates from around a millennium later. Around 2000 BC a new race appeared that buried their dead in short cists of stone slabs and one was discovered at Whitestone in the parish of Skene. With the introduction of bronze came the practice of cremation and the ashes of the dead were placed into an urn. One of the finest examples *in the whole province of Mar* was discovered at Leuchar Brae also in the parish of Skene. These examples of the early Bronze Age are preserved in the museum at Marischal College in Aberdeen. There are many examples of stone circles, also from the Bronze Age, in and around both parishes including the standing stones at Cullerlie which unusually are situated on low ground. About 400 BC iron was introduced and an impressive relic of this age is the hill fort known as the Barmekin of Echt. It consists of five concentric lines of defence with originally an entrance which would have zig-zagged through the defence system thus increasing the difficulty of forcing a passage. Some urns and a sword dating from the time of the Roman invasion were discovered in the early 1800s near Kirkville in the parish of Skene, but there is no evidence of Roman occupation in the area, their camps of Raedykes near Stonehaven, Normandykes near Culter and Glenmailen at Ythan Wells all lying further to the south and east. A few remains of the early Celtic church survive including some Christian symbols added to the standing stone at Nether Corskie near Dunecht and an incised cross which was found at Upper Mains of Echt.

In the twelfth and thirteen centuries there was a move away from the loosely knit tribal organisation into a strictly organised feudal system with the granting of the lands by the crown to what were to become powerful families. The lands of Skene were erected into a Burgh of Barony in 1317 when Robert de Skene received a charter from Robert the Bruce. The family owned the lands of Skene till 1827. The lands of Echt passed through various hands until in the early 15th century the Forbes family took ownership. The estate was erected into a Barony by Mary, Queen of Scots, in 1565 but not before one of the earliest events of the Reformation, the burning of Church of Echt in 1558 and the battle of Corrichie in 1562. The battle was fought between forces commanded by George Gordon, Earl of Huntly, and the forces of the Queen led by her half-brother Lord James Stewart, the Earl of Moray. Huntly had been offended by the Queen who had revived the old Earldom of Mar and handed over its lands, which had been within Huntly's influence, to her half-brother. Huntly gathered his followers and prepared to march on Aberdeen where Moray's army were garrisoned. On the day before the battle Huntly's troops had reached the Loch of Skene where they spent the night. Moray, having learned of Huntly's plan, had sent an advance party out to head off the attack and on reaching Garlogie set up camp for the night. The opposing forces were now within striking distance of one another and when Huntly realised he was going to be outnumbered he withdrew west to the Hill of Fare. It was there that the battle was fought on 28 October 1562. The fighting was soon over and resulted in the defeat and death of Huntly, the Cock of the North. The Queen was in Aberdeen at the time and not present at the battle, but two features are marked on Ordnance Survey maps namely Queen Mary's Chair where tradition claimed she watched the battle and Queen Mary's Well from which it was supposed she drank. The Deeside Field Club marked the spot of the battle in 1952 when Viscount Arbuthnott, Her Majesty's Lord Lieutenant, unveiled a twelve foot granite pillar with a Gaelic inscription *Cuimhnichibh La Coire Fhraoichidh* – Remember the day of Corrichie.

The old road from Aberdeen through Skene is particularly interesting and some of it no longer narrow and with the rough surface of former days, is still in use. On leaving Aberdeen the road headed west along what is now Rosemount Place, Mile End and Mid Stocket. From there the road followed the line of the Lang Stracht, now much altered, before reaching Kingswells where it disappears except for a short stretch behind Kingswells House. It reappears a little further west at the crossroad leading to the old Quaker burial ground. When a new route into the city to the south was constructed Dr. Francis Edmond built a cottage obstructing the old road thus preventing it being used any longer as a route leading to Kingswells. The old road however can still be seen continuing westwards and enters the parish of Skene at Brodiach, originally an old coaching inn, the Six Mile House. Here at one time, and built into a dyke, was an unusual sundial made from a large boulder with a smoothed sloping face for the dial and the date 1790 in large figures below. On the gnomon was engraved the name Jos. Allan and the date once again. Several years ago when Brodiach was sold the then owner moved the sundial to his new house a short distance away where it can still be seen today. The old road continues until it reaches Kirktown of Skene (more commonly referred to as Kirkton of Skene), a distance of about three miles, and even beyond traces can still be found all the way to Dunecht.

In 1803 the new turnpike road was built which is still the main road today. Over the years it has seen many upgrades and improvements. Originally the turnpike extended only as far as the tollhouse at Leddach and it took another six years before agreement was reached on extending the road to Dunecht and on to Alford. During the nineteenth century this road was used for the mail coaches among them the *Aberdeen and Alford Telegraph* and the *Skene Star Coach*. Sometime later other major roads were built serving the two parishes of Skene and Echt. Today the old turnpike road divides just as it enters the parish of Skene, one branch following the 1803 road with Westhill on the north and continuing on through Elrick to Dunecht. The other branch, more to the south, runs through Garlogie to the boundary with the parish of Echt where it divides again the branch to the north leading to Echt and the more southerly branch passing through Cullerly (now usually spelt Cullerlie) to the old Wicker Inn and Raemore Raemoir).

When the Deeside Railway was opened in 1853 there was a move to build a branch line of some twenty miles from Coalford, a mile west of Peterculter, to pass through Echt but it never came to fruition. Around 1870 another rail link to Aberdeen was under consideration. The plan was to start from Bucksburn on the Great North line and cross the valley to Brodiach. It would then follow the south side of that road to Leddach and from there to Netherton and the Mills of Garlogie and on to Echt. It was also suggested that it could be extended along the north side of the Loch of Skene to Dunecht. But nothing came of this proposal or the one of 1907 when it was suggested that a light railway be constructed from Aberdeen to Echt, which would also serve Skene. It was then left to local bus services to provide the transport links to Aberdeen.

GOODALLS MOTOR AND CYCLE WORKS
ECHT

In addition to the bus services that James Goodall ran, he also owned a number of garages in the area. He also ran taxi services and provided car hire for weddings.

Leaving Aberdeen by the Old Skene road, Kinmundy lies a little distance to the north on the eastern edge of Westhill. The House of Kinmundy is built on much older foundations which may well have been of religious significance. Like so many other houses and castles in the north east Kinmundy has its ghost, the Green Lady, but her story has long since been forgotten. The house is well-named because its literal meaning is the *head of a hill lying above a moor*.

The Old Skene road next reaches Westhill which less than fifty years ago was but a straggling line of little crofts and cottages with a small school. In 1955 the roll of the school was 43. It had at one time been a larger community with its own bakery and a flourishing joiner's business. The hamlet had been called Blackhills and the name was painted on several of the old pew doors of Skene Church before its renovation in 1932. In 1859 when the properties of Blackhills and Wester Kinmundy were bought by a John Anderson it is said that he took *west* from one name and *hill* from the other to make the new name *Westhill*. In 1963 an Aberdeen solicitor Ronald Fraser Dean with the backing of the former Aberdeen District Council, the Secretary of State for Scotland and supported financially by Ashdale Land and Property Company Ltd. set out plans for the creation of a new satellite town, the Westhill of today. Since the construction of the first houses in 1968 it has undergone rapid expansion. A reminder of the old village is the first post office situated on the eastern edge of the town now replaced by a more convenient one in the shopping centre. The old house now serves a very different purpose as Berriedale Funeral Home.

Until the rapid development of Westhill, Elrick village was the hub of the local community and it was there in the early 20th century that we would have found the grocer, the shoemaker, the blacksmith and the joiner and even a cycle repair shop. The original name of the village and that shown on the postcard was Earlick. The derivation of the name may come from the Gaelic *eilreig* meaning a place where deer were driven for hunting. The original name can still be found on the name of the cottages on the right hand south side of the Straik Road on the A944 just beyond the garage. All that remains of these earlier days of Elrick is a farrier's business which still operates from one of the cottages. The road as seen here is still fairly rough and it remained so until the late 1920s.

Broadstraik, Skene

The turnpike road shown here runs parallel to the old Skene Road which is still used but of course is now well surfaced. The old road passes the shopping centre of Westhill to the north and soon reaches one of its highest points where once the old Broadstraik Inn stood. Mains Cottage replaced the inn and it was there that the shoemaker Mr. Howitt had his business.

Some of the stones from the old inn were used to build the new Wayside Inn of Broadstraik at Elrick on the lower turnpike road which in 1903 was bought by Alexander Craigmile and demolished to make way for the new Broadstraik Inn. It was completed in 1905 at a cost of £1105 and is built in the style of an old English inn. The following is taken from an account of a wedding reception held in the inn at the beginning of the 20th century - *the men headed for the bar, which had fitted seats at the bay window. In front of the bar counter were spittoons and sawdust for pipe smokers and a steel bar to rest feet.*

Leddach House, formerly always called The Leddach, is on the north of the A944 opposite the new Leddach Grange housing development. The name is derived from *leth-davach*, a land measurement with a meaning of *half the townland*, a fair interpretation considering the estate was once some 700 acres. It was at one time owned by Alexander Crombie who was one of the subscribers to the new turnpike road of 1803. The original road went as far as Leddach where there was a toll gate. The present house was built by Peter Jamieson a blacking manufacturer who owned a factory in Aberdeen and later in 1937 it was bought by Doctor Junor who carried on his practice from the house for the next 30 to 40 years.

Mason Lodge Buildings and Post Office, Skene

Mason Lodge is situated further west on the A944 where in 1824 St. George's Lodge of Freemasons was constituted. When the Lodge closed the hall was converted into dwelling houses but the little community still bears the name.

Mason Lodge

PROCTOR'S ORPHANAGE, SKENE.

The Proctor Orphanage situated a short distance north east of the Kirkton of Skene and just off the Old Skene Road was built in 1893 with a legacy of £4,500 left for the purpose by James Proctor of Kirkville, Skene. Boys and girls, usually ten to twelve in number were brought up as a family under the care of a house father and mother. Jessie Kesson (Jessie Grant Macdonald) who was to become a well-known writer was born in Inverness Workhouse on 29 October 1916 and brought up in Elgin. In 1927 her mother was convicted of neglect and Jessie was sent to Proctor's Orphanage. She attended Skene School and left the orphanage in 1932 to go into service, but suffered a nervous breakdown. She was then sent to a croft at Abriachan near Loch Ness where she met Johnnie Kesson, a cattleman whom she married in 1937. Her book *The White Bird Passes*, which tells the story of her childhood, was dedicated to Donald Murray the dominie of Skene School. The orphanage was used as a set when the book was made into a film in 1980. Latterly the house was known as Proctor's Childrens' Home. It has been disused for some time but kept watertight. The trustees are at present considering *proposals that would aim to keep it in a use that would be as close, as modern practices allow, to the donor's original intentions.*

KIRKTON OF SKENE FROM THE CHURCH GATE

The Old Skene Road goes directly into the Kirkton of Skene and over the years the village has changed very little. A recent description states that it *consists of a main road through its centre that branches off into a small warren of five or so streets that service just under 100 houses, a pub - The Red Star Inn, a big playpark, a village hall, the church and George Ogg and Sons the local shop.* The additional housing was built on the former glebe lands behind what was the old manse and which is now a private house known as Kirkstane House. J McIntosh is the name above the door of what is now the Red Star Inn and at the top of the road is the smiddy once a busy place with its dark interior, its big bellows and glowing fire but it closed in the 1930s.

This view looks from the smiddy towards the church with what is now George Ogg's shop on the right. Early in the last century it was owned by George McPetrie.

A church existed in Skene as early as 1296 and was dedicated to St. Bride but no trace remains except perhaps for an old belfry which is in the garden of Easter Skene House. The present church was built in 1801 and is a typical square building of the period. The church then had seating for 700 and in the *New Statistical Account* of 1843 the writer, the local minister the Rev. George Mackenzie, mentions that the church was rather small because in the period from the building of the church in 1801 to 1841 the population of the parish had increased from 1,140 to 1,846. In 1932, when the Rev. John McMurtrie was the minister, the church had a complete renovation which reduced its seating capacity to around 400. Outside the church is an interesting relic of former days, a mortsafe. The mortsafe was constructed in iron and stone and is of great weight. It would have been placed over the coffin for about six weeks then removed for further use when the body inside was sufficiently decayed, thus preventing it being stolen to be sold to anatomy students. The war memorial to those of the parish who lost their lives in World War I stands in front of the church and was unveiled in 1921. After the monument was complete it was discovered that one of the men listed was still alive and the name had to be chiselled out. On the right is the North Lodge of Kirkville House which was bought by Lord Cowdray in 1924. On the chimney breast can be seen the entwined Cs of Lord Cowdray and his wife Annie whose maiden name was Cass.

Milne Hall, Skene

The Milne Hall in the Kirkton was opened in 1835 and over the years the hall has had extensive additions and improvements. There are two references to the name of Milne in the *New Statistical Account* of 1843 and in all probability the hall is named after one of them. Dr. Milne of Bombay is reported as leaving a bequest of £20 yearly for the *teaching of twenty five poor scholars* and Mr. Milne of Fornet of Skene kept some of his best oxen which were sent to the London market from the port of Aberdeen.

Kirkville House stands about a quarter of a mile south of the Kirkton of Skene and was built in 1826. Captain Grant of Kirkville was the prime mover in a proposal to erect a monument to commemorate the first Reform Bill of 1832. Money ran out before the tower could be erected and interest faded. The Reform Bill Monument has been on OS Maps since 1869 and the remains can be seen on the farm of Burnside on the Hill of Carnie just south of Mason Lodge. G M Fraser in his book *Historic Walks* published in 1927 described it thus: *It is in the form of a semi-circle set against a stone dyke: six courses of hammer-blocked masonry have been built all round the semi-circle, to a height of six feet; a central foundation had been constructed as a base for the monument proper. Great numbers of gathered stones are piled on this general foundation.* Kirkville Estate was greatly improved after Lord Cowdray bought it in 1924. Today the house is a nursing home.

1843 was a momentous year in the history of the established Kirk in Scotland when the right to call a minister was challenged. This led to what has been called the Disruption when many of the church members broke away to form their own free kirk. It happened here in Skene and thus was established the Free Church and Manse built barely a mile from the Parish Church on the Aberdeen to Alford road overlooking the loch. Attendance at church was the norm in these days and a strange superstition is recalled in the *Statistical Account* of Skene written in 1952. *Sixty years ago a young mother, proud of her first baby, carried him over to her neighbour's house. But she was not asked to come in, instead the older woman told her, kindly but firmly, Noo, dinna gang ony wey else till yeve been at the kirk*. The church was later to become Skene United Free Church and in 1929 when most of the Free churches were again united with the old parish church it became Lochside Church. When its minister, the Rev. T Allison, retired in 1941 the two congregations united under the Rev. John McMurtrie. The Lochside buildings were sold to a local man who converted the manse into two dwelling houses and the church, now with its spire removed, into a workshop

The present house of Easter Skene which stands about a quarter of a mile northwest of the Kirkton, was built in 1832 by William McCombie who succeeded his father in 1824. The architect was John Smith (Tudor Johnny), Aberdeen's City Architect, who was responsible for the building of many of the granite buildings of the city earning it the nickname of *The Granite City*. In around 1840 William McCombie of Easter Skene and Lynturk (not to be confused with his cousin, also William McCombie, of Tillyfour) founded a fine herd of Aberdeen Angus cattle which became famous and gained many of the highest honours at the big agricultural shows. It was the oldest established herd of the breed in Aberdeenshire in the 1870s and 1880s. By the time William McCombie died in 1890 he had made great improvements to the estate and reclaimed much waste marsh and moorland. The estates of Easter Skene were purchased from the family in 1924 and now form part of the Dunecht Estate. On the north face of the Hill of Auchronie on the lands of Easter Skene and close to the side of the road stands the Drum Stone with its inscription *Drum Stone, Harlaw, 1411*. The stone recalls the Battle of Harlaw, fought three miles west of Inverurie, between Donald, Lord of the Isles, who was intent on invading Aberdeen and the Earl of Mar who rallied the local landowners, including Sir Alexander Irvine of Drum, to repel the attack. On a clear day, both the tower of Drum and the Harlaw battlefield are visible. It was at this spot, according to tradition, that Sir Alexander Irvine of Drum, who was to lose his life at the battle, gave instructions to his family and servants in the event of his death.

In the north of the parish lies the village of Lyne of Skene with its shop and the then various modes of transport very much in evidence. The local shop could be relied on to stock most of the needs of the locals but this was supplemented by the shop using its own horse and cart delivery service as shown on the left. Notice too the donkey cart on the right. Lyne of Skene is pronounced the *Line of Skene* by the locals. The word comes from the Gaelic *loinn*, a meadow, field or enclosure. James Macdonald in his *Place Names of West Aberdeenshire* suggests it means a line or straight row of houses, which was probably a good description of the village. The old name for the village was Hatton, the *toon*, namely the town, nearest the *ha'*, the big house. The houses of the period would still have had their open kitchen fireplaces with their white-washed sides and black iron sway for pot and girdle and would have used peat as the fuel. There was a plentiful supply to be cut on the peat mosses nearby and every house had its peat stack.

At the start of the 1900s there were at least three smithies in the neighbourhood at Kirkton, Broadstraik and here at Lyne of Skene. In those days the smithy or *smiddy* was kept busy with horses to be shod or fitted with *sharps* in the winter for the icy roads. The wandering packman William Chisholm visited the Lyne in 1854 and was so taken by the place that he settled down. Before his death in 1862 he wrote the poem *The Bodies o' the Lyne o' Skene* in which he captures what life was like at the time. In particular the two lines

There's tailors, souters, wrights an' smiths,
Like brithers, kind ha'e been to me

illustrate just how busy the village once was. Alas the smiddy has now shut its doors for the last time and the horse and cart of a century ago has been replaced by the busy motorised traffic that passes through the village on its way from Kintore to Dunecht.

A proud farmer with his fine pair of Clydesdales. The Clydesdale horse is the pride of Scotland and is a native breed which was founded in Lanarkshire – Clydesdale being the old name for the district. The history of the breed dates back to the middle of the 18th century when Flemish stallions were first used to give the breed greater weight and substance. The *Third statistical Account* of Echt written in 1950 mentions that *the Echt, Skene and Midmar Agricultural Association has its headquarters at Echt where it holds its annual show in July where there is usually a large entry of livestock. Until recently annual hoeing and ploughing matches took place. To see 30 pairs of horses at work in a field was an inspiring sight and one could not but admire the splendid work done, but the motor tractor now dominates the local ploughing match.* How sad it is that we now hardly ever see a pair of working Clydesdales.

SKENE HOUSE

The Skene family are said to have been a sept of the Clan Robertson. According to tradition a younger son of Robertson of Struan saved the life of King Malcolm Canmore by killing a wolf with his sgian, or knife. The king then granted him as much land as could be covered by a hawk's flight, which included the Loch of Skene. In 1318 Robert de Skene, who is regarded as the first baron of Skene, received a charter from Robert the Bruce. The charter and the sgian were at one time kept in the charter chest at Skene House. The arms of the Skenes are three sgians supported by three wolves' heads. Notice the stone wolf statue which can be seen on the right. The suggestion that the name Skene is derived from the *sgian* is now generally assumed to be untrue and Fenton Wyness the eminent Aberdeen historian suggests the name is probably of Pictish origin from *sgain* meaning *thorn*. The great chestnut at Skene House mentioned in the *New Statistical Account* of 1843 can be see on the left and the weight of the lower branches have over the years been bent to the ground where they have taken root.

The old fourteenth century Tower of Skene although much altered still forms the north wing of Skene House and has the distinction of being the first stone and lime house in Mar, and the oldest occupied residence in all Aberdeenshire. According to account in the New Spalding Club (1887) it was *originally built of three arches or stories, and entered by a ladder on the second storey. It was covered with a mound of earth upon the top of the third arch, and is built with lime, quite run together or vitrified, and the walls about ten feet thick. It continued in its original state till about the year 1680, that (sic) the arches being taken out, it was roofed and floored by Jean Burnet, Lady Skene, Relict of John Skene of that ilk, in her widowhood, and makes now part of the accommodation of the present house.* Lady Skene also built a large addition, now the middle part of the house, *the family having always lived before that in low thatch houses, like the better kind of their common farm houses.* The south wing, balancing the old tower, was added about 1745, and the entire house was remodelled between 1847 and 1850.

The family owned the lands of Skene till 1827 when the last of the direct line Alexander Skene, the 20th Laird, died at the age of 60 having been a deaf mute since birth. This sad end to an ancient line was traditionally attributed to a curse pronounced on the family. The succession to the estate fell to his nephew James Duff, 4th Earl Fife. He was the son of Alexander the 3rd Earl who had married Mary Skene the eldest daughter of George Skene of that ilk, the 18th Laird. In 1798 Balmoral had been bought by James Duff the 2nd Earl Fife, but in 1852 it was sold to Prince Albert by James Duff who in 1857 succeeded his uncle and became the 5th Earl Fife. In that year he was created a peer with the title Baron Skene of Skene. In 1880 the house and estate were rented to George Hamilton by his son Alexander Duff, the 6th Earl Fife, who married Princess Louise granddaughter of Queen Victoria in 1889, and was created Duke of Fife. In 1896 he built Mar Lodge on the estate which had been bought in 1735 by William Duff who later became the 1st Earl Fife. This was the family's first foothold on Deeside and it was owned by them until the 1960s. It has been suggested that the sgian given to the family with the charter in 1318 may have been moved to Mar Lodge when the house was rented. Skene House and estate was finally bought in 1905 by George Hamilton's son Brigadier General John G H Hamilton. The lands were sold by him in 1921 to Lord Cowdray who purchased the greater part including the Loch of Skene. The Hamilton family sold the house sometime after World War II.

Skene House

Skene House Stables.

The stable block of Skene House, a large two storey granite built in a baronial style with a battlemented centre clock tower, dates from around 1860 and was designed by Archibald Simpson. The stables had stalls for at least a dozen horses and two coach houses as well as a harness room. In addition accommodation was provided for the two coachmen. The stable block was converted in 1984 to form five houses.

THE GARDENS, SKENE HOUSE

The walled garden of Skene House dates from around 1847 to 1850 and at one time contained fruit trees, shrubs herbaceous borders and some large greenhouses. The gardens were looked after by a head gardener who was assisted by two full-time gardeners and some other part-time workers. The gardens became a market garden in 1950 but were closed as such in 1980.

In the dead of winter the Loch of Skene can be a dark and forbidding place. This has given rise to all sorts of superstitions and it is said that those who dare to venture to the loch side can gaze out at what appear to be a mysterious set of curved tracks embedded in the ice, tracks which seem to have been made by a coach or carriage. Legend has it that it is a reminder of the day that Auld Nick paid a visit to his devil-worshipping friend the Wizard Laird of Skene. The 16th Laird lived from about 1680 to 1724 and learnt the mastery of the black arts while a student in Padua. It is said he made a pact with the devil. His coachman called Kilgour was ordered one night to prepare the coach and horses to transport a guest from Skene House. He was told that on no account was he to turn round and look at the stranger. The Laird ordered him to take the direct route across the Loch of Skene. There had been one night's frost and the coachman thought the journey would be impossible, but he was told not to worry the ice would hold. Kilgour's curiosity, however, got the better of him just as he was about to reach the far bank of the loch and he turned round and saw Auld Nick in the coach. As soon as he saw him the ice cracked, the devil turned into a raven and flew away, and the coach and horses sunk to the bottom of the loch. Superstition still lives on and for many years thereafter fires were lit at Hallowe'en to keep the devil at bay. W. Somerset Maugham, while convalescing from tuberculosis at Nordrach-on-Dee in Banchory, wrote a short story called *The Magician* in which evil deeds take place at Skene House .

Boathouse, Loch of Skene.

On the north side of the Loch of Skene is one of the gateways to Dunecht House. It consists of two high tower lodges in Scots baronial style flanking tall wrought iron gates and to the rear a boathouse with portcullis gate. The gateway was built in 1922-23 to the design of A Marshall MacKenzie, the well-known Aberdeen architect. The Loch of Skene is on the western edge of the parish of Skene and is fed by the Kinnernie Burn, and drained by the Leuchar Burn. It is the loch which gives Skene its beauty and character. Trees and marshy ground surround it, and it is a well-known resort of wild birds. The loch abounds with pike and eels, and all attempts to eliminate them in favour of trout have proved unsuccessful. In the 1920s the loch was raised some three feet from its natural level to provide hydro-electric power. Lord Cowdray also created several artificial islands in the loch which were used as butts for duck shooting.

To the south of The Loch of Skene and powered by the Leuchar Burn was the old wool mill at Garlogie. The mill which dates from before 1830 was taken over in that year by Messrs. Hadden & Sons of Aberdeen. *The New Statistical Account* of 1843 reports that the mill had a work force of about 120 of all ages. Steam power was occasionally used when the supply of water from the Loch of Skene fell short. Gas was introduced in 1843 so that the employees could continue their work in the dark days of winter. The company were very attentive to the needs of the workers and provided cottages for their accommodation. There was also a school which was attended by the younger children during the day and by the older children and adults in the evening when their long working day at the mill was over. The distance to the parish church in Skene prevented the families having regular attendance and thus the school became a place of worship on Sunday evenings. The mill closed in 1904 and a water turbine was installed in the 1920s to generate electricity. Garlogie, it is claimed, may have been one of the first Aberdeenshire villages to have its own electricity.

In 1931 the south wing of the building was converted into Garlogie Hall. In 1994-5 a Museum of Power was created by conversion of the engine house and turbine hall. One of the exhibits was the original beam engine which powered the mill in its early days and the only one to have survived intact in its original location. Because of staffing shortages the museum is at present closed.

The Garlogie Inn dates back to the 1800s when it was a *Port & Ale House*, a stop over point for coachmen to water their horses and have a wee dram, before heading on to Echt or Deeside. This was the forerunner of the Garlogie Bar. When the wool mill was still in operation Garlogie would have been a busy place; not only would the old inn have provided a meeting place for the locals but the shop next door, owned in the early days of the last century by Robert Allan, would have provided the families with all their needs The shop has long since closed and Woodbine Cottage has been incorporated into the Garlogie Inn which has recently been extended providing a very popular stopping place for the tourist.

THE HOTEL, ECHT.

Leaving the parish of Skene and moving west the B 9119 leads to Echt. The hotel is shown here as *The Balcarres Arms*. At the time of its building the Earl of Crawford and Balcarres, who had bought the estate of Dunecht in 1845, was the local landowner. It was not until the estate had been sold to Weetman Dickinson Pearson, later to become Lord Cowdray, that the name was changed to *The Cowdray Arms*. The garden of the hotel was the old market stance. The former schoolhouse is the imposing building on the left. The name Echt has been spelt in various ways such as Eych and Hachtis in a charter dated 1220, Heych in 1226, Eych in 1274, and Eycht in 1638. Echt is popularly known as the Vale or Howe of Echt and it has therefore been suggested that the name is a modification of a Gaelic word *eoch* or *eocht* meaning *a howe*. Fenton Wyness suggests that *Eych* is a personal name and could have been the builder of the Barmekin hill fort. In the *New Statistical Account* of 1842 a very different interpretation is given of the name. It is said to have been derived from the Gaelic word *each* meaning *a horse* and refers to an occasion when a division of an ancient Caledonian army were camped in the parish close to the Barmekin of Echt in a time of a severe drought. The men, in desperate need of water to drink, noticed that when one of their horses was scratching the ground with his feet some signs of water were discovered. A well was dug at the spot and the army was saved from dying of thirst. In memory of that event, this particular district, and afterwards the parish was given the name of Echt.

The war memorial of Echt stands between the church grounds and the new churchyard and was designed by William McMillan of Aberdeen. It is a bronze statue of a Gordon Highlander in full battle dress on a base of granite from Dunecht Quarry and was unveiled on 6 November 1921. The memorial for the men of the parish who fell in World War II is an oak tablet placed in the vestibule of the church and was unveiled on 21 December 1947. Close by in the churchyard is the memorial to Lord Cowdray (1856- 1927) and his wife Annie Cass (1860-1932). The old manse of Echt is now a private house known as Glenecht and the new manse is on the opposite side of the road.

War Memorial, Echt.

E. C. Manse, Echt

The pupils of Echt in the very early 1900s pose for the photographer outside the school. The school, which dates from the 1870s, would originally have been the parish school and hence the church style windows. Notice the neat dress of the youngsters. Katie Johnson was a proficient seamstress who died in the very early 1900s aged 95. She lived in Whitehills Cottage, near Sunhoney, and devoted her life ensuring that the young girls of the parish developed their sewing skills. Some of the clothes worn by the boys and girls in the picture may well have been made as a result of her tuition. The playground shelters can be seen in the background and some have survived to this day. At one time Echt provided education for pupils up to the age of fourteen, at that time the school leaving age. In September 1955 Echt School had three full-time teachers, one part-time, three visiting teachers and a roll of 60. A generous education authority at that time provided bicycles for children who lived more than three miles from the school.

On the right a later view of the post office in Echt which is also shown on the previous page but note that the house now has an upper floor. Today the house still remains but without the thatch which has been removed. The post office is now in the village shop at the west end. The original post office was opened in 1840 and at the time was known as the penny post office. Rowland Hill had campaigned for Post Office reform in the late 1830s and penny post was introduced in May 1840 when the first postage stamp, the Penny Black, was issued to be used on all letter mail. The gable end of the Aberdeen Town and County Bank, later the Clydesdale Bank and now closed can be seen further up the road on the right. The church wall is on the other side of the road and before the days of motorised transport churchgoers would stable their horses in the hotel stables where now the village hall (*the Cowdray Hall*) has been built.

Sandison's Bakery and General Merchant shop in Echt in the early part of the last century. The shop had a bake house to the rear of the shop and the aroma of freshly made bread was a feature in Echt in those days. The *Third Statistical Account* of Echt written in 1950 states that *Echt has a school, a sub-post office, a bank, a police station, a garage, and a general merchant's shop which is a branch of the SCWS with a bakery attached.* The school remains but only as a primary school; the original sub-post office has closed; there is no longer a bank, police station or garage; the Scottish Co-operative Wholesale Society has closed as has its bakery, but the shop still remains and since around 1965 has had a sub-post office.

The Gordon Highlanders in camp at Echt in the early 1900s. They were billeted in the familiar bell tents of the time and crowds of Sunday visitors came to view the camp. The camp may well have been in the fields near the old Mill of Echt close to where there was at one time a shooting range. In the background on the first card is the village of Echt and on the other the Hill of Fare. One soldier in particular (JS) was missing the lady of his life and on 27 June 1907 posted this message to Miss N Tough of Dufftown:

When the golden sun is shining
And your thoughts from care are free
When on olden times you're thinking
Sometimes, Darling, think of me.

A feature of both Echt and Dunecht which still survive to this day are the houses built by the laird for the workers of the estate. The neat line of houses in Echt was built in the early 1900s during the time of A C Pirie's ownership of Dunecht Estate. The long low building in the centre background was the store for the general merchant's shop. On the right the imposing house, now called Kirkton Station House, was the police station. In former days the water supply for Echt came from springs in the fields above Upper Mains Farm. The villagers drew their water from two pumps, one at the police station and the other opposite the entrance to the new churchyard. Lord Cowdray later built a large reservoir on the Hill of Fare which replaced the old water supply.

The Forbes family of Echt originally stayed at the Castle of Echt which was just beyond the present house at Auld Echt. Fourteen generations of the family stayed in the district from around the mid 15th century. The family bought Housedale, a small estate now in the centre of Dunecht Estate, and started adding to the existing house. It is possible to date when the family moved to Housedale by the plaque on the garden wall with the date 1687 and the initials AF and EI i.e. Arthur Forbes, and Elizabeth Innes. On the wall of the house a cartouche inscribed with a Latin inscription, the date 1705 and the initials AF and KM i.e. Arthur Forbes and his wife Katharine Melville whom he married in 1696 on the death of his first wife. The estate was sold in 1726 to William Duff, Lord Braco who in 1759 became Viscount Macduff and Earl Fife (styled thus rather than Earl of Fife) in the Irish Peerage. The family home was Duff House near Banff, built by the 1st Earl but he, and later his family, loaned money to estates in the northeast, often eventually acquiring them. Housedale was bought for his son Alexander, who was later to become the 3rd Earl Fife. He did a lot of work on the new estate such as planting trees and starting cultivation of lazy beds some of which can still be seen at Dunecht. The Duffs sold it back to the Forbes family in 1801. William Forbes, the then head of the family, found Housedale to be too small and decided to build a larger house. This was the present Dunecht House, at the time known as Echt House. Housedale became the home of the head gardener and the walled garden dating from about 1820 was to become famous for its fruits and flowers. The estate employed up to twenty gardeners and William Smith, head gardener for many years during the last century, was responsible for the layout of the Dunecht golf course in the grounds of the estate. He will also be remembered for his contributions to gardening radio programmes and his weekly reports in the local press. His son Ronald Smith was brought up in Housedale and went on to have a distinguished gardening career.

In 1845 the 7th Earl of Balcarres and 24th Earl of Crawford bought the house as a Scottish seat for his family, the Lindsays, who had been amassing wealth from the Lancashire coalfields. It was at this time that the name was changed to Dunecht House. Three years later the house became the home of his heir, Lord Lindsay. William Smith, the Aberdeen architect, was commissioned in 1859 to produce plans to redesign the original house and draw up plans for the building of the tower connecting the original house with the extensive additions. The formal gardens in front of the house were originally laid with box hedges and parterres ornamented by specimen conifers. These were later removed and replaced by colourful herbaceous borders and summer planting. The garden as shown here is crisscrossed by paths following very precise lines with yew trees spaced out on the edges. On the death of his father in 1869 Lord Lindsay inherited the titles. He was a keen amateur astronomer and built an observatory nearby at Craig-na-loaigh. The observatory, completed in 1872, was a square building with a balustrade around the top built on one of the highest points on the estate with a clear view of the Barmekin which also had equipment linked with Dunecht. George Washington Wilson. the famous Aberdeen photographer, became involved with him and took some very early photographs of the moon. After the death of the Earl this fine observatory was dismantled and placed at the disposal of the nation. The instruments and magnificent astronomical library were moved to the observatory on Blackford Hill, Edinburgh, where part of the gift can still be seen.

In 1867 George Edmund Street was commissioned to design the chapel at Dunecht House. The commission was not easy and Lord Lindsay was not best pleased with the time it took to complete it, caused he claimed by Street's desire to supervise every part of the building work. The completed chapel, however, was stunning, some 50 feet high and 100 feet long with its great round arch leading to the chancel. In 1880 Lord Lindsay, now the 8th Earl of Balcarres and 25th Earl of Crawford, died while in Florence and his embalmed body sealed in a heavy coffin was transported back to Aberdeen. From there it was taken by road during a violent snowstorm and laid to rest in the vault of the chapel. In December 1881 it was discovered that his body had disappeared. Rumours started to circulate on what had happened to the remains of the Earl and it was not until July 1882 that the body was found in a shallow grave about 500 yards from Dunecht House. Later the Dowager Lady Crawford erected a small granite cross with inscription at the spot where the body was found. Charles Soutar, a local rat catcher who was also a poacher, was given a five year prison sentence for the theft but when he was released he denied the crime and, it is said, named the real criminals. In 1886 the estate was offered for sale. In 1897 it was proposed to convert Dunecht House into a boys' college to rank with Eton, Rugby and Harrow for the education of sons of gentlemen. A company was formed and directors appointed, among whom were the Right Hon. The Earl of Moray and Sir William Geddes, Principal of Aberdeen University, but the project never materialised. In 1899 the estate passed into the hands of Mr Alexander Charles Pirie of Craibstone, Aberdeen, a well-known Aberdeen paper manufacturer.

THE LIBRARY, DUNECHT HOUSE.

In 1867 George Edmund Street was also commissioned to design a great library at Dunecht for Lord Lindsay. The 120 foot library was a most imposing room *designed of railway-station proportions, but in the non-pejorative sense, in that these were the cathedrals of the Victorian age*. The room had a spectacular Italian marble chimneypiece and long galleries down either side. The ceiling was barrel vaulted with roof lights. It was never used to house Lord Lindsay's vast book collection and in the late 1920s the room was converted into the Ballroom.

In 1907 Weetman Dickinson Pearson rented the estate from A C Pirie who was finding it difficult to finance the upkeep of the estate. Three years later Pearson bought the house and estate. He was born in 1856 and by 1900 was the owner of S Pearson & Son, originally a small building firm in Yorkshire. By 1900 the company employed 20,000 men building railways, docks, harbours, waterworks and drainage systems in Britain, Ireland, Mexico and China. Pearson was elected Liberal M.P. for Colchester in 1895 and held the seat until 1910. Dunecht House became the family's chief country residence and Sir Aston Webb was commissioned to make further changes to the house which was furnished luxuriously. In 1916 Pearson was given the title Viscount Cowdray of Midhurst. Their family seat is now Cowdray House which sits on a 16,500 acre estate in West Sussex. Dunecht House was stripped of much of its grandeur and part was converted into flats shortly after World War II. The chapel too was stripped of all its beuty and the crypt is now a double garage. The estate is spread over 53,000 acres in Aberdeenshire and Kincardineshire and is managed from Dunecht on behalf of the Pearson Family Trust by Charles Pearson, the youngest son of the late 3rd Viscount Cowdray. Among the properties owned are Dunnottar Castle Estate (including the castle) near Stonehaven, Birse Castle on Deeside and Edinglassie Estate in the Cairngorms National Park.

Shown here is a fine view of Dunecht House, a mixture of Scottish baronial, Palladian and Victorian architecture with bow windows, round turrets and a tower with lancet windows opening onto small balconies on the upper levels. When A C Pirie bought the house and estate he employed G Bennet Mitchell to design two further additions, a new dining room and a conservatory. The conservatory can be seen on the right of the picture.

The Dunecht Estate Office and Hall were designed by Dr. William Kelly and were completed in 1927. The hall on the east side, with its large Venetian window, provides an excellent venue for local events. On the outside wall of the office there is an imposing armorial plaque. The supporters are particularly unusual; they are on the dexter side (the left) a man in a diving suit, and on the sinister side (the right) a figure in sandals and a fringed poncho intended as a Mexican peon (labourer). These are the arms of Viscount Cowdray who became an extremely rich man from the money he made from exploiting Mexico's first oil production under the dictator Porfirio Diaz. His extensive interests in Mexico, from construction of railways, dams, harbours and tunnels to mining and manufacturing, from rural estates to his ownership of the El Aguila oil company, meant that he was often absent from the House of Commons where he served as an M.P. and thus earned the nickname *The Member for Mexico*.

NORTH GATES, DUNECHT HOUSE

The gateways at the entrances to Dunecht Estate are a particular outstanding feature and on page 30 the east gate is shown. The north entrance, regarded as the main gate, leads off from the village of Dunecht. Set back from the road it has gryphons set on top of the two rusticated granite piers and fine wrought iron gates. The entrance was designed by William Kelly and dates from 1924-25. Previously the road ran through part of the estate at this point and was re-routed to take account of the new entrance.

The Dunecht Estate had its own dairy and dairy herd. The Home Farm with its dairy is said to date from the early 18th century, but over the years the dairy has been extensively remodelled. The high standards of the dairy are very evident; the dairymen, well turned out, are standing by with the milk pails at the ready. Latterly the dairy was used for the rearing of pheasants. Lord Cowdray renovated many of the farm houses and steadings on the estate equipping them with all modern conveniences. As well as taking a keen interest in all of the needs of their estate workers the Cowdrays were good benefactors to other causes. They made a generous donation, not only to the new Sick Children's Hospital in Aberdeen which Lady Cowdray opened in 1928, but also to the fund set up for the building of Aberdeen Royal Infirmary which was opened by the Duke and Duchess of York in 1936. In addition they gave Aberdeen its impressive Cowdray Hall with the War Memorial frontage unveiled by King George V in 1925. Lord Cowdray died in May 1927 only a few days before he was due to receive the Freedom of the City.

The scene is a picnic held at Scotstown Moor on the Dunecht Estate possibly in 1907. The children look to be on their best behaviour and are sitting on the ground possibly in keen anticipation of the arrival of the picnic food. By the dress of the adults it would suggest that the picnic was arranged by Lord and Lady Cowdray for the youngsters of the estate workers. In that year the Cowdrays had rented the property from A C Pirie. The message on the reverse of the postcard is also interesting and offers a remedy for idle hands! It reads: *I have arrived home again alright. I enjoyed my holiday fine. I hope you are enjoying yourself and doing a bit of your sock. I did a lot of crocheting. I was not allowed to sit idle as Mary said it was not good for me. We will be seeing you soon. Love from Will.*

The village of Dunecht was formerly known as Waterton and was renamed Dunecht about the same time as Echt House was renamed Dunecht House - from the Gaelic *dun* meaning *the fort* of Echt. In the early 1900s A C Pirie commissioned the architect G Bennet Mitchell to design sizeable cottage-style houses for estate workers. The houses had projecting porches and dormers. The house on the right called Derncleugh with the pitched roof was made up of two shops, a restaurant and next door James Mutch, cycle agent. The old road is seen to pass in front of the houses. This property was given a new frontage in 1923 and a chemist shop and garage were added adjoining the property.

Dunecht in the early days of the last century had a full range of shops. On the left is the butcher and shoemaker's shop built in 1923. The bus operated by James Mutch is at the door and the two village policemen are seen standing with their bicycles appearing to be in deep conversation. At the time the village had, in addition to the butcher and shoemakers, a chemist, a general merchant, a sub-post office and a garage with a shop attached selling sweets and cigarettes. The garage and chemist shop can be seen on the far right of the picture and were built in 1925. A feature of both Echt and Dunecht is the excellent state of the houses built by the estate in the early part of the last century. Over the years the houses have been modernised as mentioned in the *Third Statistical Account* written in 1950. *The present Lord Cowdray makes housing one of his special interests and has greatly improved farm house and steadings on his estate. Most have electric light but where there is none paraffin lamps are used. Calor or rural gas is also in common use. The old fashioned fireplace with the crook has almost disappeared and even the kitchen range is seldom seen. The triplex grate and the Rayburn stove are very popular. Coal, which at present costs £5 a ton, is in general use; logs supplement the coal, but they are expensive, costing £3 to £3 10/- per ton. Peat is still used, but not so extensively as formerly. The houses, usually of the cottage type, with three or four apartments, are in excellent condition; there are no one-roomed houses. The average number of people to a house is four.*

This card shows the north side of the village of Dunecht with, on the left, the old farmhouse and with the two cyclists at the door, the low roof of the bothy or chaumer as it was known in this area. The chaumer with a bed and a kist to hold their possessions would have been used by the unmarried male farm workers. Their food was prepared by the farmer's wife. Full-time agricultural labour in the area was scarce and many farms employed labour on a monthly engagement. The Dunecht Estate farms were more fortunate and their farm workers usually remained for many years in their jobs.

Further along the road was the post office and on the opposite side of the road the drystane dykes, a signatory feature of Dunecht Estate and shown clearly on the opposite page. This dyke was built in the time of Lord Cowdray but in the middle of the last century George Davie, a stone dyker of the time, is said to have built miles of the walls around the estate having first having walked up to ten miles to his work.

Sometime later the post office also became the general merchant's shop in Dunecht owned by J Lessell. He also ran a lorry for coal deliveries. Next door was the public bar. Up to the middle of the last century the outlying parts of both the parishes of Skene and Echt were served by a continuous stream of merchant vans including butchers, bakers, grocers and fish men.

Sometime in the early 1970s the shop became a SPAR store part of a world wide supermarket chain linking independant wholesalers and retailers designed to use collective purchasing power to offer the best deal to consumers. The company *De Spar* was founded in Holland in 1932 by Adriann Van Well. The name comes fom the acronym of the Dutch sentence <u>D</u>oor <u>E</u>endrachtig <u>S</u>amenwerken <u>P</u>rofiteren <u>A</u>llan <u>R</u>egelmatig which translates into *We all benefit from joint co-operation*. SPAR has become synonymous with Van Well's fir tree which is still today the instantly recognised company logo. After further changes of ownership the shop finally closed and the post office business was transferred to the garage in Dunecht. The property is now a private house.

The message on the card provides a good example of how, in the early part of the last century, a postcard rather than the telephone was used as the means of communication. The card was written at Knockquharn, a farm situated a short distance east of Dunecht House and close to the Loch of Skene. The halfpenny stamp (then the inland postal rate for a postcard) has the postmark of Dunecht on 9 August 1910. The card did not have to travel far as it was sent to a Miss Wilson of Brode Shade (sic), now known as Broadshade, which is just north of the Old Skene Road a short distance to the east of Kirkton of Skene. The message is:

Dear Jennie,
I will be over on Sunday first be sure and be at home.
Yours
Mary Matthew

The farm implement on the cart is a *neep barra* or turnip sower. The name on the side of the cart is *William Davidson, Gardener, Hilton* and it could well be William holding the horse's reins. Whether the *Hilton* refers to the Hilton, a district in Aberdeen, or is the name of a local farm is not known.